Me and My Friends

I Can Be a Friend

written by Daniel Nunn

illustrated by Clare Elsom

raintree

brary
ue

D0334472

30131 05363784 6

LONDON BOROUGH OF BARNET

Raintree is an imprint of Capstone Global Library Limited,
a company incorporated in England and Wales having
its registered office at 7 Pilgrim Street, London, EC4V 6LB –
Registered company number: 6695582

www.raintreepublishers.co.uk
myorders@raintreepublishers.co.uk

Text © Capstone Global Library Limited 2015
First published in paperback 2015
The moral rights of the proprietor have been asserted.

All rights reserved. No part of this publication may be
reproduced in any form or by any means (including
photocopying or storing it in any medium by electronic
means and whether or not transiently or incidentally to
some other use of this publication) without the written
permission of the copyright owner, except in accordance
with the provisions of the Copyright, Designs and Patents
Act 1988 or under the terms of a licence issued by the
Copyright Licensing Agency, Saffron House, 6–10 Kirby
Street, London EC1N 8TS (www.cla.co.uk). Applications
for the copyright owner's written permission should be
addressed to the publisher.

Edited by Brynn Baker
Designed by Steve Mead and Kyle Grenz
Production by Helen McCreath
Original illustrations © Clare Elsom
Originated by Capstone Global Library Ltd
Printed and bound in China by LEO

ISBN 978 1 406 28161 3 (hardback)
18 17 16 15 14
10 9 8 7 6 5 4 3 2 1

ISBN 978 1 406 28166 8 (paperback)
19 18 17 16 15
10 9 8 7 6 5 4 3 2 1

British Library Cataloguing in Publication Data
A full catalogue record for this book is available from
the British Library.

Contents

Being a friend

I share with my friend.

Good friends share.

I take turns with my friend.

Good friends take turns.

I tell the truth to my friend.

Good friends tell the truth.

I listen to my friend.

Good friends listen.

I care for my friend.

Good friends care.

I help my friend.

Good friends help.

I play nicely with my friends.

Good friends play nicely.

I have fun with my friends!

Good friends have fun!

Being friendly quiz

Which of these pictures shows being friendly?

Did being friendly make these children happy? Why?
Do you like being friendly?

Picture glossary

care to look after your friends and help them to be happy

friend person you care about and have fun with

share to divide something up between you and your friends or take turns using it

Index

Notes for teachers and parents

BEFORE READING

Building background: Ask children to describe what makes a good friend. How do they make friends? What's the best thing about having a friend?

AFTER READING

Recall and reflection: Ask the class how children in the book had fun. What things do they like to do? (Playing a game, jumping a rope.) Do the children in the book look happy? How can they tell?

Sentence knowledge: Choose a page, and ask children to identify a capital letter and a full stop. Why is there a capital letter? What does a full stop signal?

Word knowledge (phonics): Ask children to point to the word *with* on page 4. Sound out the three phonemes in the word *w/ i/ th.* Ask children to sound out each phoneme as they point at the letters, and then blend the sounds together to make the word *with.* Ask them which of these words have the same sound in the middle: *pin, pan, bit, but, ten* or *tin.*

Word recognition: Look at the word *nicely* on page 17. Help children to clearly hear the two syllables (*nice/ ly*). Say the word slowly while clapping once for each syllable.

AFTER-READING ACTIVITIES

Ask children to work with partners to draw a picture of something they like to do with good friends. They can write a sentence or dictate a sentence about the picture. Bind the pages into a class book about friendship.

In this book

Topic
friendship

Topic words and phrases
care
friends
have fun
help
play
share
take turns
tell the truth

Sentence stems
I ___ for my friend.
I ___ to my friend.
I ___with my friend.
Good friends ___.

High-frequency words
for
have
I
my
the
to
with